## BEING WITH GOD

A Bible and prayer guide
for people with dementia

# WORDS OF
# HOPE

Also in the **Being with God** series: *Words of faith, Words of peace*.

Copyright © Scripture Union 2010

ISBN: 9781844275205

Scripture Union, 207–209 Queensway, Bletchley,
Milton Keynes, MK2 2EB, England
Email: info@scriptureunion.org.uk
Website: www.scriptureunion.org.uk

Scripture Union USA, PO Box 987, Valley Forge, PA 19482, USA
Email: info@scriptureunion.org
Website: www.scriptureunion.org

Scripture Union Australia, Locked Bag 2, Central Coast Business Centre,
NSW 2252, Australia
Website: www.scriptureunion.org.au

Scripture quotations, unless otherwise indicated, are taken from the HOLY BIBLE,
NEW INTERNATIONAL VERSION. Copyright © 1973, 1978, 1984 by International
Bible Society. Anglicisation copyright © 1979, 1984, 1989, 1995, 1996, 2001.
Used by permission of Hodder & Stoughton Ltd.

British Library Cataloguing-in-Publication Data: a catalogue record of this book
is available from the British Library.

Developed and edited by 'Tricia Williams
Expert consultant and introduction: Margaret Goodall
All recordings produced by Gordon Lorenz

Cover design and internal layout by Martin Lore
Printed and bound in Singapore by Tien Wah Press Ltd

Scripture Union is an international Christian charity working with churches
in more than 130 countries providing resources to bring the good news of Jesus
Christ to children, young people and families and to encourage them to develop
spiritually through the Bible and prayer. As well as coordinating a network of
volunteers, staff and associates who run holidays, church-based events and school
Christian groups, Scripture Union produces a wide range of publications and
supports those who use their resources through training programmes.

'DRAW NIGH TO GOD,
AND HE WILL
DRAW NIGH TO YOU.'

*James 4:8, KJV*

FOR VALERIE AND DAVID

# CONTENTS

---

# FOREWORD

———

Dementia is a cruel robber. It robs people of their memory, their personality, their ability to recognise and react normally even with partners and family they've loved for years. In short, it robs them of themselves and the life they've known. Confusion and strangeness replace the familiar and safe. They have a whole lifetime of experience and knowledge behind them – yet that knowledge is tantalisingly beyond their mind's grasp.

The knowledge which escapes them may well include a lifelong faith in God and a love of his word in the Bible which has been a constant source of strength and reassurance during challenging times in the past. However, with the onset of dementia, that comfort is lost to them as much-loved biblical stories, prayers and hymns are frustratingly hard to remember.

With its carefully chosen mix of familiar words and evocative music, this imaginative and practical resource is nothing less than a Godsend – a nudge to the memory which at its most obvious level is a delightful way to aid conversation and recall, but at its deepest, opens, for the person with dementia, a real connection to faith and the God who has never stopped loving them.

**Pam Rhodes**
Presenter of BBC's Songs of Praise,
Patron of Methodist Homes for the Aged

# WELCOME
# AND THANKS

We hope that you will find this Bible and prayer guide brings you God's blessing and comfort – whether you are the person with dementia or you are a 'carer'.

This resource has been developed specifically for people with dementia, but older people who are struggling with memory loss may also find it helpful.

We are so grateful for the help and encouragement of many in the creation of this resource. **Margaret Goodall**, Chaplaincy Advisor for **MHA**, has given constant encouragement as our expert consultant. We've also much appreciated help and advice from **Christian Council on Ageing** and **Alzheimer's Society**. Individuals facing the challenges of dementia have given invaluable feedback on the content. We are especially grateful for the support and encouragement of **Pam Rhodes**, presenter of BBC's **Songs of Praise**, Patron of MHA.

Our thanks too to all those who have given towards the development of these resources – including: MHA, Christian Council on Ageing and Social Interface Ltd – whose generosity has helped enormously in the creation of this resource.

## Words of hope: the CD

With its familiar hymns and evocative performances, this CD has been specially produced and compiled for inclusion in this guide. It would not have been possible without the generous support of Gordon Lorenz, music producer, and of the professional and highly gifted performers he has brought together. Our thanks to all of those who have been involved in these recordings, and for their great creativity and sensitivity in bringing us this music.

Our prayer is that – as you use this guide – you will know that God is close to you, as you draw near to him.

**'Tricia Williams**
Editor

# INTRODUCTION

## A WORD FOR CARERS

Some older people, either because they are living with dementia or because of age, are no longer able to join in public worship. The following pages offer a way to help them reconnect with the Christian faith and story.

People with dementia are sometimes thought of as no longer being able to worship. But even when people have not spoken for a while – as those involved in their care will know – they are still able to join in with familiar prayers and hymns. We need to offer clues as to what is going on, a context for worship, and cues in the words that are so familiar, in order to help them join in.

As the effects of dementia increase, it is more difficult to interact with others and to be understood. But while thoughts and words may be confused, feelings and emotions experienced are still real. So if we can meet people on an emotional or 'feeling' level instead of the rational or thinking level, then we meet people who are like us but who need help to be part of the world around them.

I hope that by using this Bible and prayer guide, people who could be isolated by dementia, will be helped to feel once again part of the Christian community, and be reminded that God loves and accepts them as they are – something we all need reminding of.

We believe in a God who can reach beyond our reasoning and understanding of words to touch us again with his love.

**Margaret Goodall**
*Chaplaincy Advisor, MHA*

# HOW TO USE
# THIS GUIDE

---

## SETTING THE SCENE

In order to use this Bible and prayer guide to best effect it will be important to 'set the scene' so that the person with dementia can recognise what is going to happen. Imagine what it's like to wake up in a strange place. For a moment all is odd and 'wrong'. For those with dementia it is always like this. So, as carers, we need to do all we can to help them focus.

Using the same setting each time we use this guide can help provide a way of 'cueing in' and be a reminder of what is about to take place. For example, a small table, with a white cloth and a Bible, cross or prayer book could make any room into the place where we regularly take time to 'be with God'. If possible, use the same Bible each time.

The same words used to introduce the session could become a familiar part of this time and again provide a cue into worship. The words need to be simple and easy to remember, affirming God's presence. For example:

God is here
*God is always here*

God is with us
*God is always with us*

## EACH DAY'S DEVOTIONAL

Each day's devotional follows a regular format which it is hoped, for some, may become a familiar prompt for this special time with God. We understand that each person with dementia (or elderly person struggling with memory loss) is an individual and will be at different stages in facing the challenges of dementia or age. For this reason, the devotionals aren't intended to be scripts. Feel free to take the suggestions here and use what is helpful or let them act as springboards to ideas and words which will help you 'come near to God' in your particular situation. Each day's outline includes:

### Prayer
The prayer at the beginning picks up on one of the themes in the Bible verses. If thanks or prayer needs are mentioned, you might like to add specific things which are known to you and relevant to your particular situation. If helpful, encourage the person you are with to join in saying the 'Amen' at the end of the prayer.

### Read
Try to use the same Bible every time you use these devotionals. If possible, choose one that the person with dementia is familiar with. It's hoped that the Bible and this booklet will be helpful cues for this time.

You might choose to use the whole Bible passage given or just the verse selection printed – whichever is easiest or most appropriate for your situation.

## Talk about...

This section aims to start you thinking and talking about the Bible verses. It picks up words and ideas from the Bible passage to prompt thinking about the themes in ways which might help bring a sense of God's presence. Choose ideas that are appropriate and helpful in your situation.

## Pray

You may like to say the Lord's Prayer each time you use one of these daily devotionals. It will probably have been familiar to many people and they may enjoy saying it aloud. It might be useful to use a traditional form of the prayer, for example:

Our Father, which art in heaven,
Hallowed be thy Name,
Thy kingdom come,
Thy will be done on earth as it is in heaven.
Give us this day our daily bread;
And forgive us our trespasses,
  as we forgive those who trespass against us;
And lead us not into temptation
    but deliver us from evil.
For thine is the kingdom, the power and
    the glory,
  forever and ever. Amen.

## Hymn or song

You might like to sing together a favourite hymn of your own choice, or listen to the suggested track from the CD – created especially for this resource – included at the back of this volume.

The CD with its wide range of music – choral, brass band, children's choirs, a gospel group and soloists – has a hymn or song (or even a chorus from Sunday school days!) which links in with the theme of each day's Bible verses. You could sing along, or invite others to come and sing with you. However you choose to use it, we hope that these evocative recordings will bring God's comfort to those using this material.

## Cues and clues box

The various suggestions are intended to act as cues and clues to the ideas and themes of the Bible verses. You might like to look at a picture, hold an object, listen to music or even paint in response to the day's devotional. Choose or adapt as most appropriate to the person with dementia, or older person, using this Bible and prayer guide.

# DAILY BIBLE READINGS

## JESUS – LIGHT AND LIFE

1 The birth of Jesus
*Luke 2:1–7*

2 The shepherds
*Luke 2:8–15*

3 The wise men
*Matthew 2:1,2,10–12*

4 The call of the disciples
*Mark 1:16–18*

5 The wedding at Cana
*John 2:1–11*

6 Jesus heals a paralysed man
*Mark 2:1–12*

7 Jesus calms the storm
*Luke 8:22–25*

8 Jairus' daughter
*Mark 5:21–24,35–43*

9 The feeding of the 5,000
*Mark 6:35–44*

10 Jesus walks on water
*John 6:16–21*

11 Jesus welcomes children
*Mark 10:13–16*

12 Jesus heals Bartimaeus
*Mark 10:46–52*

13 Jesus meets Zacchaeus
*Luke 19:1–10*

14 Jesus enters Jerusalem
*John 12:12–16*

15 The Last Supper
*Mark 14:12–26*

16 Jesus is crucified
*Luke 23:26,27,32–34*

17 The thief on the cross
*Luke 23:39–43*

18 The death of Jesus
*Luke 23:44–47*

19 Christ is risen
*Luke 24:1–8*

20 On the road to Emmaus
*Luke 24:13–16,28–32*

21 Jesus returns to heaven
*Luke 24:50–53*

## PSALMS – WORDS OF HOPE

22 'Blessed is the man…'
*Psalm 1:1–3*

23 'The LORD is my shepherd'
*Psalm 23:1–6*

24 'The LORD is my light and my salvation'
*Psalm 27:1–6,14*

25 'Blessed is he…'
*Psalm 32:1,2,11*

26 'I will extol the LORD at all times'
*Psalm 34:1–7*

27 'I waited patiently for the LORD'
*Psalm 40:1–3*

28 'God is our refuge and strength'
*Psalm 46:1–7,10,11*

29 'Have mercy on me, O God'
*Psalm 51:1,2,7–12*

30 'I lift up my eyes to the hills'
*Psalm 121:1–8*

31 'O LORD, you have searched me…'
*Psalm 139:1–4,13–16*

# JESUS – LIGHT AND LIFE

These well-loved words from the Bible tell of Jesus' life – from Christmas to Easter – his disciples and the people they met. As we listen to these Gospel readings, we too can meet with Jesus who brings us his light and life.

# THE BIRTH
# OF JESUS

## CUES AND CLUES

Some of the following
might help as you read
today's verses from the
Bible and pray.

### Pictures
Christmas cards
showing the wise men;
the wise men presenting
their gifts; a star.

### Objects
Gifts; a star.

### To do
If it's possible, look at the
stars together; or, open
some small gifts together;
or, depending on your
situation, ask some
volunteers from your
local church to perform a
short nativity play.

**PRAYER**

Lord God, thank you for sending your Son Jesus
into our world. Thank you that you are with us
now. *Amen.*

**READING** Luke 2:1–7

**While they were there, the time came for
the baby to be born, and she gave birth to her
firstborn, a son. She wrapped him in cloths
and placed him in a manger, because there
was no room for them in the inn.**
Luke 2:6,7

**TALK ABOUT...**
- ☐ The birth of a baby; special times
- ☐ The Christmas story; Christmas
- ☐ Where you are living now
- ☐ Jesus, a human being like us
- ☐ Jesus, with us now

**PRAY**
'Our Father, which art in heaven...'

**HYMN OR SONG**
'Away in a manger'
(CD, *Words of hope*, track 1)

# THE SHEPHERDS

**CUES AND CLUES**

Some of the following might help as you read today's verses from the Bible and pray.

**Pictures**
Christmas cards showing the shepherds; Bethlehem; angels.

**Objects**
Sheepskin rug; a 'toy' sheep to hold; a Christmas tree 'angel'.

**PRAYER**
We praise you heavenly Father for the good news of Jesus. Help us to know your peace and joy. *Amen.*

**READING** Luke 2:8–15

**And there were shepherds living out in the fields near by, keeping watch over their flocks at night. An angel of the Lord appeared to them, and the glory of the Lord shone around them … But the angel said to them, 'Do not be afraid. I bring you good news of great joy that will be for all the people. Today in the town of David a Saviour has been born to you; he is Christ the Lord.'**
*Luke 2:8–11*

**TALK ABOUT…**
☐ Shepherds and sheep; being busy
☐ Angels
☐ Receiving good news
☐ Christmas
☐ The baby Jesus; God coming to us where we are

**PRAY**
'Our Father, which art in heaven…'

**HYMN OR SONG**
'While shepherds watched their flocks by night' (CD, *Words of hope*, track 2)

# THE
# WISE MEN

## CUES AND CLUES

Some of the following
might help as you read
today's verses from the
Bible and pray.

**Pictures**
Photos of babies –
children of family or
friends; Christmas card
nativity scenes; fine art
prints of nativity scenes.

**Objects**
A nativity scene.

**PRAYER**
Lord Jesus, we offer our lives to you today and
worship you as King. *Amen.*

**READING** Matthew 2:1,2,10–12

**Magi from the east came ... and asked, 'Where
is the one who has been born king of the Jews?
We saw his star in the east and have come to
worship him.' ... On coming to the house, they
saw the child with his mother Mary, and they
bowed down and worshipped him. Then they
opened their treasures and presented him with
gifts of gold and of incense and of myrrh.**
*Matthew 2:1,2,11*

**TALK ABOUT...**
☐ The nativity scene
☐ Looking at the stars
☐ School Christmas plays
☐ Gifts – receiving and giving
☐ What God has given to you

**PRAY**
'Our Father, which art in heaven…'

**HYMN OR SONG**
'We three kings of Orient are'
(CD, *Words of hope,* track 3)

# THE CALL OF
# THE DISCIPLES

---

**PRAYER**

Lord Jesus, thank you that you are with us now. Help us to hear your words. *Amen.*

**READING** Mark 1:16–18

**As Jesus walked beside the Sea of Galilee, he saw Simon and his brother Andrew casting a net into the lake, for they were fishermen. 'Come, follow me,' Jesus said, 'and I will make you fishers of men.' At once they left their nets and followed him.**
*Mark 1:16–18*

**TALK ABOUT...**

- ☐ A time when you were walking on a beach
- ☐ A time when you went fishing
- ☐ The story of Jesus on the beach calling the fishermen to be his followers
- ☐ Jesus, speaking to you

**PRAY**

'Our Father, which art in heaven...'

**HYMN OR SONG**

'I will make you fishers of men' (CD, *Words of hope*, track 4)

# THE WEDDING AT CANA

---

## CUES AND CLUES

Some of the following might help as you read today's verses from the Bible and pray.

### Pictures
Family and friends' wedding photos; a photo of Cana in Galilee.

### Objects
A wedding invitation; a wine bottle (or non-alcoholic alternative, eg red grape juice); a large stone pot or jar.

### PRAYER
Lord Jesus, please help us and meet our needs today. Thank you that you give us good things. *Amen.*

### READING John 2:1–11

**On the third day a wedding took place at Cana in Galilee. … When the wine was gone, Jesus' mother said to him, 'They have no more wine.' … Nearby stood six stone water jars … Jesus said to the servants, 'Fill the jars with water' … Then he told them, 'Now draw some out and take it to the master of the banquet.' … the master of the banquet tasted the water that had been turned into wine. … 'Everyone brings out the choice wine first and then the cheaper wine … but you have saved the best till now.'**
John 2:1–10

### TALK ABOUT…
- ☐ Weddings
- ☐ Miracles
- ☐ Asking Jesus for help
- ☐ Good things God has given you

### PRAY
'Our Father, which art in heaven…'

### HYMN OR SONG
'Now thank we all our God'
(CD, *Words of hope*, track 5)

# JESUS HEALS A
# PARALYSED MAN

## CUES AND CLUES

Some of the following
might help as you read
today's verses from the
Bible and pray.

### Pictures
Jesus healing someone
(eg fine art, or picture
in Bible storybook); a
picture of someone in a
wheelchair.

### Objects
A few roof tiles; a
walking stick or frame.

### PRAYER
Lord Jesus, thank you for friends and family who
help me; doctors, nurses and all who care for
me. Lord, you know all our needs – please bring
us your comfort today. *Amen.*

### READING Mark 2:1–12

**Some men came, bringing to him a paralytic,
carried by four of them. Since they could not
get him to Jesus because of the crowd, they
made an opening in the roof above Jesus and,
after digging through it, lowered the mat the
paralysed man was lying on.**
Mark 2:3,4

### TALK ABOUT...
- ☐ Crowds
- ☐ People who help us and care for us
- ☐ If helpful, being ill and what makes
  us feel better
- ☐ Forgiveness

### PRAY
'Our Father, which art in heaven…'

### HYMN OR SONG
'Praise my soul the King of heaven'
(CD, *Words of hope*, track 6)

# JESUS CALMS
# THE STORM

---

## CUES AND CLUES

Some of the following might help as you read today's verses from the Bible and pray.

### Pictures
A small sail or rowing boat; a storm at sea; sunrise over the sea.

### Objects
A model or toy boat; a cross (to remind you that Jesus is with you).

### PRAYER
Lord Jesus, thank you that you are with us in difficult times. Help us to know your calm. *Amen.*

### READING Luke 8:22–25

**One day Jesus said to his disciples, 'Let's go over to the other side of the lake.' So they got into a boat and set out. As they sailed, he fell asleep. A squall came down on the lake … and they were in great danger. The disciples went and woke him, saying, 'Master, Master, we're going to drown!' He got up and rebuked the wind and the raging waters; the storm subsided, and all was calm.**
*Luke 8:22–24*

### TALK ABOUT…
☐ Storms you've experienced (at sea; on land)
☐ The calm after a storm
☐ Knowing Jesus is with you in difficult times

### PRAY
'Our Father, which art in heaven…'

### HYMN OR SONG
'Will your anchor hold in the storms of life?'
(CD, *Words of hope*, track 7)

# JAIRUS' DAUGHTER

## CUES AND CLUES

Some of the following might help as you read today's verses from the Bible and pray.

### Pictures
Photos of children, or yourself as a child; a picture of Jesus healing Jairus' daughter (eg from a Bible storybook).

### Objects
A birthday card with the number '12' on it.

### To do
If appropriate, take the hand of the person with whom you are reading at verse 41.

### PRAYER
Lord God, help us not to be afraid. Thank you that we are in your hands. Help us to trust in you. *Amen.*

### READING Mark 5:21–24,35–43

**While Jesus was still speaking, some men came from the house of Jairus, the synagogue ruler. 'Your daughter is dead,' they said. 'Why bother the teacher any more?' ... Jesus told the synagogue ruler, 'Don't be afraid; just believe.' ... he ... went in where the child was. He took her by the hand and said to her, *'Talitha koum!'* (which means, 'Little girl, I say to you, get up!'). Immediately the girl stood up and walked around (she was twelve years old).** *Mark 5:35,36,40–42*

### TALK ABOUT...
☐ Childhood illness
☐ The kindness of Jesus
☐ Knowing that God is with you now

### PRAY
'Our Father, which art in heaven...'

### HYMN OR SONG
'Gentle Jesus, meek and mild'
(CD, *Words of hope,* track 8)

# THE FEEDING
# OF THE 5,000

## CUES AND CLUES

Some of the following
might help as you read
today's verses from the
Bible and pray.

### Pictures
Photos of a family or
church picnic.

### Objects
Bread rolls and fish (eg
sardines); sandwiches;
a picnic basket.

### To do
Share lunch; or, if easy
in your situation, have
a picnic.

### PRAYER
Lord Jesus, thank you for the food you provide
for us. Please give us everything we need today.
*Amen.*

### READING Mark 6:35–44

**Then Jesus directed them to have all the
people sit down in groups on the green grass.
… Taking the five loaves and the two fish and
looking up to heaven, he gave thanks and
broke the loaves. Then he gave them to his
disciples to set before the people. He also
divided the two fish among them all. They all
ate and were satisfied … The number of the
men who had eaten was five thousand.**
*Mark 6:39,41,42,44*

### TALK ABOUT…
- ☐ Having a picnic
- ☐ Providing food for others (eg Christmas
  dinner, a picnic, parties)
- ☐ What God has given you
- ☐ Thanking Jesus for what he's given you

### PRAY
'Our Father, which art in heaven…'

### HYMN OR SONG
'Break thou the bread of life'
(CD, *Words of hope*, track 9)

# JESUS WALKS ON WATER

## CUES AND CLUES

Some of the following might help as you read today's verses from the Bible and pray.

### Pictures

Photos of people rowing a boat; a storm at sea; the Sea of Galilee.

### Objects

Sandals (to suggest Jesus walking on the water); a boat paddle or oar (if one is readily available!); an inflatable rubber ring.

**PRAYER**

Lord Jesus, thank you for being with me now. Help us to hear your words of peace now. *Amen.*

**READING** John 6:16–21

**When evening came, his disciples went down to the lake, where they got into a boat and set off across the lake for Capernaum. … A strong wind was blowing and the waters grew rough. When they had rowed three or three and a half miles, they saw Jesus approaching the boat, walking on the water; and they were terrified. But he said to them, 'It is I; don't be afraid.'** John 6:16–20

**TALK ABOUT…**

☐ Rowing a boat
☐ Being at sea in a storm
☐ Being scared
☐ Knowing Jesus hears our prayers and is with you

**PRAY**

'Our Father, which art in heaven…'

**HYMN OR SONG**

'King of glory, King of peace' (CD, *Words of hope*, track 10)

# JESUS WELCOMES CHILDREN

**PRAYER**

Lord Jesus, thank you that you welcome us into your presence. Lord, help us to know your blessing today. *Amen.*

**READING** Mark 10:13–16

**People were bringing little children to Jesus to have him touch them, but the disciples rebuked them. ... He said to them, 'Let the little children come to me, and do not hinder them, for the kingdom of God belongs to such as these.'**
*Mark 10:13,14*

**TALK ABOUT...**
☐ Families and friends of all ages
☐ Being a small child
☐ Jesus welcomes children
☐ God's love for all people

**PRAY**
'Our Father, which art in heaven...'

**HYMN OR SONG**
'Jesus loves me this I know'
(CD, *Words of hope*, track 11)

# JESUS HEALS BARTIMAEUS

---

## CUES AND CLUES

Some of the following might help as you read today's verses from the Bible and pray.

**Pictures**
Beggars; people in need.

**Objects**
A 'begging bowl';
a white stick.

**PRAYER**
Lord Jesus, thank you that you hear us when we call out to you. You know what our needs are – help us to bring them to you now. *Amen.*

**READING** Mark 10:46–52

**As Jesus and his disciples ... were leaving the city, a blind man, Bartimaeus ... was sitting by the roadside begging. ... he began to shout, 'Jesus, Son of David, have mercy on me!' ...**

**'What do you want me to do for you?' Jesus asked him. The blind man said, 'Rabbi, I want to see.'**

**'Go,' said Jesus, 'your faith has healed you.' Immediately he received his sight ...**
Mark 10:46,47,51,52

**TALK ABOUT...**
- ☐ Not being able to see very well – your own experience, or that of people you know
- ☐ How Jesus wants to help us with our needs and problems
- ☐ God hears us when we call out to him

**PRAY**
'Our Father, which art in heaven...'

**HYMN OR SONG**
'To God be the glory'
(CD, *Words of hope*, track 12)

# JESUS MEETS ZACCHAEUS

## CUES AND CLUES

Some of the following might help as you read today's verses from the Bible and pray.

### Pictures
Photos of trees; someone climbing a tree (eg someone pruning a tree); crowds.

### Objects
A tax return form; money.

### To do
Point out trees that you can see from your window. If able, go outside and sit under a tree for today's Bible reading and prayer.

## PRAYER
Lord Jesus, thank you that you know us by name. Help us to hear your words today. *Amen.*

## READING Luke 19:1–10

**Jesus entered Jericho and was passing through. A man was there by the name of Zacchaeus; he was a chief tax collector and was wealthy. He wanted to see who Jesus was, but being a short man he could not, because of the crowd. So he ran ahead and climbed a sycamore-fig tree to see him … When Jesus reached the spot, he looked up and said to him, 'Zacchaeus, come down … I must stay at your house today.'**
*Luke 19:1–5*

## TALK ABOUT…
☐ Zacchaeus' story
☐ Being short (or tall)!
☐ Climbing trees
☐ Your name
☐ God calls you by name

## PRAY
'Our Father, which art in heaven…'

## HYMN OR SONG
'Zacchaeus was a very little man'
(CD, *Words of hope*, track 13)

# JESUS ENTERS JERUSALEM

## CUES AND CLUES

Some of the following might help as you read today's verses from the Bible and pray.

### Pictures
Public celebrations (eg soldiers returning from war, royal marriages, a coronation etc); a Bible storybook picture of Jesus riding into Jerusalem on a donkey.

### Objects
A Palm Sunday cross.

**PRAYER**
Praise God for sending his Son Jesus – our King. Lord Jesus, we welcome you. *Amen.*

**READING** John 12:12–16

**The next day the great crowd that had come for the Feast heard that Jesus was on his way to Jerusalem. They took palm branches and went out to meet him, shouting,**
  **'Hosanna!'**
  **'Blessed is he who comes in the name**
    **of the Lord!'**
  **'Blessed is the King of Israel!'**
*John 12:12,13*

**TALK ABOUT...**
- ☐ Public celebrations (eg soldiers returning from war, royal marriages etc)
- ☐ Palm branches; Palm Sunday
- ☐ Jesus riding on a donkey
- ☐ Celebrating Jesus' presence with us

**PRAY**
'Our Father, which art in heaven...'

**HYMN OR SONG**
'Ride on, ride on in majesty'
(CD, *Words of hope*, track 14)

# THE LAST SUPPER

## PRAYER

Lord Jesus, thank you for inviting us into your presence. Help us to welcome you into our lives. *Amen.*

## READING Mark 14: 12–26

**While they were eating, Jesus took bread, gave thanks and broke it, and gave it to his disciples, saying, 'Take it; this is my body.' Then he took the cup, gave thanks and offered it to them, and they all drank from it. 'This is my blood of the covenant, which is poured out for many,' he said to them.**

*Mark 14:22–24*

## TALK ABOUT...

☐ Having a special meal with friends
☐ The Lord's Supper (or 'Communion' – or whichever term you're most used to and comfortable with)
☐ Jesus – he gave his life for us
☐ Jesus – with us now

## HYMN OR SONG

'My song is love unknown'
(CD, *Words of hope*, track 15)

# JESUS IS CRUCIFIED

---

## CUES AND CLUES

Some of the following might help as you read today's verses from the Bible and pray.

### Pictures
Any fine art print of Jesus on the cross, or other picture of the cross.

### Objects
A cross.

## PRAYER

Lord Jesus, thank you for giving your life for us on the cross. Thank you, Lord God, for your forgiveness because of Jesus. *Amen.*

## READING Luke 23:26,27,32–34

**As they led him away, they seized Simon from Cyrene ... and put the cross on him and made him carry it behind Jesus. ... When they came to the place called the Skull, there they crucified him, along with the criminals ... Jesus said, 'Father, forgive them, for they do not know what they are doing.'**
Luke 23:26,33,34

## TALK ABOUT...
☐ Jesus being crucified
☐ The Good Friday story and reminiscences
☐ Jesus forgives us

## PRAY
'Our Father, which art in heaven...'

## HYMN OR SONG
'When I survey the wondrous cross'
(CD, *Words of hope*, track 16)

# THE THIEF ON
# THE CROSS

---

## CUES AND CLUES

Some of the following
might help as you read
today's verses from the
Bible and pray.

### Pictures
Jesus on the cross, or the
thieves being crucified
with Jesus, or the three
crosses.

### Objects
A cross.

**PRAYER**
Lord Jesus, thank you for the hope we have
in you. *Amen.*

**READING** Luke 23:39–43

**Then he said, 'Jesus, remember me when you
come into your kingdom.' Jesus answered him,
'I tell you the truth, today you will be with me
in paradise.'**
*Luke* 23:42,43

**TALK ABOUT...**
- ☐ Crime and punishment
- ☐ Jesus taking our punishment on the cross
- ☐ Jesus forgives us
- ☐ Jesus' promise of our being with
  him in heaven

**PRAY**
'Our Father, which art in heaven...'

**HYMN OR SONG**
'Amazing grace'
(CD, *Words of hope*, track 17)

# THE DEATH OF JESUS

---

## CUES AND CLUES

Some of the following might help as you read today's verses from the Bible and pray.

**Pictures**
Any fine art print of Jesus on the cross, or other picture of the cross.

**Objects**
A cross.

**PRAYER**
Father God, we commit our lives to your care, knowing that we can trust you. *Amen.*

**READING** Luke 23:44–47

**It was now about the sixth hour, and darkness came over the whole land … for the sun stopped shining. And the curtain of the temple was torn in two. Jesus called out with a loud voice, 'Father, into your hands I commit my spirit.' … The centurion, seeing what had happened, praised God and said, 'Surely this was a righteous man.'**
Luke 23:44–47

**TALK ABOUT…**
- ☐ Missing someone you knew and loved
- ☐ Jesus trusted in God at the darkest time in his life
- ☐ The Roman soldier and his response to Jesus
- ☐ Jesus – what he means to you

**PRAY**
'Our Father, which art in heaven…'

**HYMN OR SONG**
'Jesus, keep me near the cross'
(CD, *Words of hope*, track 18)

# CHRIST
# IS RISEN

## CUES AND CLUES

Some of the following
might help as you read
today's verses from the
Bible and pray.

### Pictures
Any photos or pictures
of the Garden Tomb
in Jerusalem; fine
art pictures of the
resurrection.

### Objects
An Easter egg;
an Easter card.

### To do
Go for a walk in the
garden; share some
Easter eggs.

**PRAYER**

Christ is risen! Hallelujah! Thank you, Lord
Jesus, that you are alive. Help us to know that
you are with us now. *Amen.*

**READING** Luke 24:1–8

**On the first day of the week, very early in the
morning, the women took the spices they
had prepared and went to the tomb. They
found the stone rolled away from the tomb,
but when they entered, they did not find the
body of the Lord Jesus. ... suddenly two men
in clothes that gleamed like lightning stood
beside them. ... 'Why do you look for the
living among the dead? He is not here:
he has risen!'**
Luke 24:1–6

**TALK ABOUT...**
☐ Easter memories
☐ Jesus is alive and with us now

**PRAY**
'Our Father, which art in heaven...'

**HYMN OR SONG**
'In the garden'
(CD, *Words of hope*, track 19)

# ON THE ROAD
# TO EMMAUS

## CUES AND CLUES

Some of the following might help as you read today's verses from the Bible and pray.

### Pictures
A Sunday afternoon walk.

### Objects
A local road or walkers' map; walking boots and walking pole.

### To do
If appropriate, you might like to bring a (well-behaved) dog along (they evoke memories and expressions of love!)

## PRAYER
Lord Jesus, open our eyes and help us to see that you are with us now. *Amen.*

## READING Luke 24:13–16,28–32

**Now that same day two of them were going to a village called Emmaus ... As they talked ... Jesus himself came up and walked along with them, but they were kept from recognising him ... When he was at the table with them, he took bread, gave thanks, broke it and began to give it to them. Then their eyes were opened and they recognised him ...**
Luke 24:13,15,16,30,31

## TALK ABOUT...
☐ Walking to places; Sunday afternoon walks
☐ Feeling sad when people (friends, family, visitors) leave us
☐ Jesus never leaves us and is with us now, hearing all we say

## PRAY
'Our Father, which art in heaven...'

## HYMN OR SONG
'He lives', from the hymn: 'I serve a risen Saviour' (CD, *Words of hope*, track 20)

## 21

# JESUS RETURNS
# TO HEAVEN

## CUES AND CLUES

Some of the following might help as you read today's verses from the Bible and pray.

**Pictures**
Pictures of celebrations; Christians in church praising God.

**Objects**
Something to bring to mind times of joy and celebration (eg streamers, confetti).

**PRAYER**
We praise you, O God, that Jesus is alive and death is defeated. Hallelujah! *Amen.*

**READING** Luke 24:50–53

**When he had led them out to the vicinity of Bethany, he lifted up his hands and blessed them. While he was blessing them, he left them and was taken up into heaven. Then they worshipped him and returned to Jerusalem with great joy. And they stayed continually at the temple, praising God.**
*Luke 24:50–53*

**TALK ABOUT...**
☐ Times when you have felt very happy; times of celebration
☐ Praising God with others (in church, at special events, with friends)
☐ Jesus is in heaven now with his Father

**PRAY**
'Our Father, which art in heaven...'

**HYMN OR SONG**
'Thine be the glory'
(CD, *Words of hope*, track 21)

# PSALMS –
# WORDS OF HOPE

Familiar words from the book of Psalms bring comfort and assurance from the God who made us and loves us. May you know his presence near you as you hear from his Word – for he is 'our refuge and strength' (Psalm 46:1).

# 'BLESSED IS THE MAN...'

## PRAYER
Thank you, Lord, for your word. Help us to hear
your words to us today. *Amen.*

## READING Psalm 1:1–3

**Blessed is the man who does not walk in the
counsel of the wicked or stand in the way of
sinners or sit in the seat of mockers. But his
delight is in the law of the LORD, and on his law
he meditates day and night. He is like a tree
planted by streams of water, which yields its
fruit in season and whose leaf does not wither.
Whatever he does prospers.**
*Psalm 1:1–3*

## TALK ABOUT...
☐ Watering your plants or gardening
☐ Reading the Bible; favourite Bible verses
   that help you
☐ What having faith in God means for you
☐ How God blesses us

## PRAY
'Our Father, which art in heaven...'

## HYMN OR SONG
'Since Jesus came into my heart'
(CD, *Words of hope*, track 22)

# 'THE LORD IS
# MY SHEPHERD ... '

---

## PRAYER
Thank you, Lord, that you are our shepherd. May
we know your care in all we do today. *Amen.*

## READING Psalm 23:1–6

**The LORD is my shepherd, I shall not be
in want. He makes me lie down in green
pastures, he leads me beside quiet waters ...
Surely goodness and love will follow me all
the days of my life, and I will dwell in the
house of the LORD for ever.**
*Psalm 23:1,2,6*

## TALK ABOUT...
☐ Sheep or lambs you have seen
☐ Jesus, the Good Shepherd, who cares for us
☐ God is always with us

## PRAY
'Our Father, which art in heaven...'

## HYMN OR SONG
'The Lord's my Shepherd'
(CD, *Words of hope*, track 23)

# 'THE LORD IS MY LIGHT AND MY SALVATION'

## CUES AND CLUES

Some of the following might help as you read today's verses from the Bible and pray.

**Pictures**
A sunrise; the sun; a castle high up on a rocky cliff.

**Objects**
A candle; a torch; attractive small rocks or stones.

**PRAYER**
Lord God, thank you that you keep us safe. Thank you that you are with us now. *Amen.*

**READING** Psalm 27:1–6,14

**The LORD is my light and my salvation – whom shall I fear? The LORD is the stronghold of my life – of whom shall I be afraid? … For in the day of trouble he will keep me safe in his dwelling; he will hide me in the shelter of his tabernacle and set me high upon a rock.**
*Psalm 27:1,5*

**TALK ABOUT...**
☐  Having light or a torch in a dark place
☐  Someone being with you in the night
    (eg a mother holding her child in the night)
☐  Being afraid
☐  Knowing that God is with you
☐  Sharing God's light with others

**PRAY**
'Our Father, which art in heaven...'

**HYMN OR SONG**
'This little light of mine'
(CD, *Words of hope*, track 24)

# 'BLESSED IS HE...'

---

## CUES AND CLUES

Some of the following might help as you read today's verses from the Bible and pray.

### Pictures
The cross; Jesus on the cross; people singing in church.

### Objects
A 'sorry' card; hymn books or familiar music books.

### PRAYER
Lord God, thank you that you forgive us our sins. Give us your peace and joy this day. *Amen.*

### READING Psalm 32:1,2,11

**Blessed is he whose transgressions are forgiven, whose sins are covered ... Rejoice in the LORD and be glad, you righteous; sing, all you who are upright in heart!**
*Psalm 32:1,11*

### TALK ABOUT...
☐ Saying sorry
☐ God forgives us – whatever our failings or wrongs
☐ Singing and being happy – God is with us

### PRAY
'Our Father, which art in heaven...'

### HYMN OR SONG
'And can it be...?'
(CD, *Words of hope*, track 25)

# 'I WILL EXTOL THE LORD AT ALL TIMES'

---

## CUES AND CLUES

Some of the following might help as you read today's verses from the Bible and pray.

### Pictures
Praying hands (eg *Praying Hands* by Albrecht Dürer); 'safe' places, rescue services; tents; people praising God.

### Objects
Simple musical instruments; hymn books or familiar music books; a Red Cross badge or sign.

### To do
If you're musical, you (and others) might enjoy playing instruments or singing now.

## PRAYER
Lord God, help us with our troubles. Give us joy, even when times are hard. *Amen.*

## READING Psalm 34:1–7

**I will extol the LORD at all times; his praise will always be on my lips. My soul will boast in the LORD; Let the afflicted hear and rejoice … The angel of the LORD encamps around those who fear him and he delivers them.**
*Psalm 34:1,2,7*

## TALK ABOUT...
☐ Being rescued from a difficult situation
☐ Camping
☐ Praising God
☐ Angels
☐ Knowing God helps us with our troubles

## PRAY
'Our Father, which art in heaven…'

## HYMN OR SONG
'O God our help in ages past'
(CD, *Words of hope*, track 26)

# 'I WAITED PATIENTLY FOR THE LORD'

## CUES AND CLUES

Some of the following might help as you read today's verses from the Bible and pray.

**Pictures**
People waiting (eg queues, bus stops); rescue services; muddy scenes; people praising God.

**Objects**
A rock; musical instruments; hymn books.

**To do**
If you're musical, you (and others) might enjoy playing instruments or singing now.

## PRAYER

Lord God, thank you that you hear us and help us when we call out to you. *Amen.*

## READING Psalm 40:1–3

**I waited patiently for the LORD; he turned to me and heard my cry. He lifted me out of the slimy pit, out of the mud and mire; he set my feet on a rock and gave me a firm place to stand. He put a new song in my mouth, a hymn of praise to our God.**
*Psalm 40:1–3*

## TALK ABOUT...

☐ Times when you've been patient or had to wait
☐ Rocks
☐ Mud (eg walking through mud in Wellington boots; childhood reminiscences)
☐ Songs of praise
☐ God hears us and will help us in our troubles

## PRAY

'Our Father, which art in heaven...'

## HYMN OR SONG

'Lord of all hopefulness'
(CD, *Words of hope,* track 27)

# 'GOD IS OUR REFUGE AND STRENGTH'

---

## CUES AND CLUES

Some of the following might help as you read today's verses from the Bible and pray.

### Pictures
Fortresses, castles, mountains; father holding frightened child; photos of home.

### Objects
A pillow or lavender-filled cushion to suggest sleep and quiet rest.

### To do
If appropriate, take the hand of the person with whom you are reading, for example, at verses 1,7,10,11.

## PRAYER
Almighty God, please help us to know you are with us today. Help us to be still and know that you are God. *Amen.*

## READING Psalm 46:1–7,10,11

**God is our refuge and strength, an ever-present help in trouble. Therefore we will not fear, though the earth give way and the mountains fall into the heart of the sea ... The LORD Almighty is with us; the God of Jacob is our fortress.**

**'Be still, and know that I am God ...'**
*Psalm 46:1,2,7,10*

## TALK ABOUT...
- ☐ Fortresses, castles, safe places
- ☐ Mountains
- ☐ Troubles or fears
- ☐ Knowing that God is with us

## PRAY
'Our Father, which art in heaven...'

## HYMN OR SONG
'O for a closer walk with God'
(CD, *Words of hope*, track 28)

# 'HAVE MERCY ON ME, O GOD'

---

## CUES AND CLUES

Some of the following might help as you read today's verses from the Bible and pray.

### Pictures
A washing powder advert (eg 'Persil washes whiter'); a picture of the prodigal son being welcomed home by his father (eg *The Return of the Prodigal Son* by Rembrandt, a Bible storybook picture).

### Objects
A familiar box of washing powder; a clean, white cotton sheet; a cross to hold.

### To do
Wash something in a bowl.

## PRAYER
Lord God, forgive us our sins. Thank you for your unfailing love and compassion. *Amen.*

## READING Psalm 51:1,2,7–12

**Have mercy on me, O God, according to your unfailing love; according to your great compassion blot out my transgressions. Wash away all my iniquity and cleanse me from my sin.**
*Psalm 51:1,2*

## TALK ABOUT…
☐ Washing
☐ God's forgiveness
☐ God accepts us – coming to God

## PRAY
'Our Father, which art in heaven…'

## HYMN OR SONG
'How sweet the name of Jesus sounds'
(CD, *Words of hope*, track 29)

# 'I LIFT UP MY EYES TO THE HILLS'

## CUES AND CLUES

Some of the following might help as you read today's verses from the Bible and pray.

**Pictures**
Photos of hills or mountains (eg Swiss holiday photos); a mother looking at her sleeping child.

**Objects**
Climbing boots; a pair of binoculars.

## PRAYER

We praise you, Lord, that you are watching over us – when we sleep, when we wake, wherever we go. *Amen.*

## READING Psalm 121:1–8

**I lift up my eyes to the hills – where does my help come from? My help comes from the Lord, the Maker of heaven and earth …**
**The Lord watches over you …**
Psalm 121:1,2,5

## TALK ABOUT…

☐ Hills, mountains
☐ God's creation – beautiful gardens, stars
☐ God is watching over us – when we sleep, when we are awake, wherever we go

## PRAY

'Our Father, which art in heaven…'

## HYMN OR SONG

'O Jesus I have promised'
(CD, *Words of hope*, track 30)

# 'O LORD, YOU HAVE SEARCHED ME...'

---

## CUES AND CLUES

Some of the following might help as you read today's verses from the Bible and pray.

**Pictures**

Photos of your everyday life and those with whom you live; family now or in the past; a baby.

**To do**

Ask a family member or friend to bring their baby to share in today's Bible reading and prayer time with you.

**PRAYER**

Thank you, Lord God, that you made me and know everything about me. *Amen.*

**READING** Psalm 139:1–4,13–16

**O LORD, you have searched me and you know me. You know when I sit and when I rise; you perceive my thoughts from afar. You discern my going out and my lying down; you are familiar with all my ways.**
*Psalm 139:1–3*

**TALK ABOUT...**

☐ Family – those who are, or were, close to us
☐ God knows everything about us – we can depend on him

**PRAY**

'Our Father, which art in heaven...'

**HYMN OR SONG**

'Come down, O love divine'
(CD, *Words of hope*, track 31)

# FURTHER
# RESOURCES

## Worship with people with dementia
'Holy, Holy, Holy': The church's ministry with people with dementia by Jackie Treetops, available from Faith in Elderly People (contact details, page 46).

The Wells of Life: Moments of worship with people with dementia by Gaynor Hammond and Jackie Treetops, available from Faith in Elderly People (contact details, page 46).

Worship for People with Dementia, a booklet based on material by Margaret Goodall, Gaynor Hammond and Laraine Moffitt, available from MHA (contact details, page 46).

## Hymns and songs
There are several good websites where you can find words and music for hymns and songs. Try: www.cyberhymnal.org

## Memory and reminiscence
Memories are Made of This: Reminiscence activities for person-centred care by Julie Heathcote, available from Alzheimer's Society (contact details, page 46).

The Memory Box by Gaynor Hammond, available from Faith in Elderly People (contact details, page 46).

Pictures to Share These books of pictures are ideal for sharing with people with dementia. Themes covered in the titles include: Childhood, Funny Old World, In the Garden, Beside the Seaside, A Sporting Life, The Countryside, A Woman's Work, Travelling, Shopping, Pets. Available from: www.picturestoshare.co.uk

## For carers and churches
In a Strange Land: People with dementia and the church by Malcolm Goldsmith, available from 4M Publications: www.4mpublications.co.uk; or: www.amazon.co.uk

# USEFUL
# CONTACT DETAILS

**MHA**
Epworth House,
Stuart Street,
Derby DE1 2EQ

01332 296200
enquiries@mha.org.uk
www.mha.org.uk

**Christian Council
on Ageing**
info@ccoa.org.uk
www.ccoa.org.uk

**Faith in Elderly People**
Publications:
Gaynor Hammond
29 Silverdale Avenue,
Guiseley,
Leeds, LS20 8BD

01943 879320
gaynor.hammond@northern.org.uk

**Alzheimer's Society**
Devon House,
58 St Katharine's Way,
London E1W 1JX

+44 (0) 20 7423 3500
enquiries@alzheimers.org.uk
www.alzheimers.org.uk

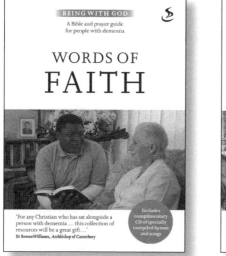
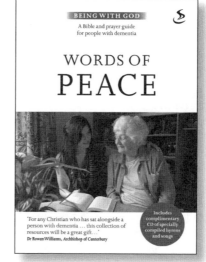

# CD:
# WORDS OF HOPE

## Hymns and songs

1 'Away in a manger'
2 'While shepherds watched their flocks by night'
3 'We three kings of Orient are'
4 'I will make you fishers of men'
5 'Now thank we all our God'
6 'Praise my soul the King of heaven'
7 'Will your anchor hold in the storms of life?'
8 'Gentle Jesus, meek and mild'
9 'Break thou the bread of life'
10 'King of glory, King of peace'
11 'Jesus loves me this I know'
12 'To God be the glory'
13 'Zacchaeus was a very little man'
14 'Ride on, ride on in majesty'
15 'My song is love unknown'
16 'When I survey the wondrous cross'
17 'Amazing grace'
18 'Jesus, keep me near the cross'
19 'In the garden'
20 'He lives', from the hymn: 'I serve a risen Saviour'
21 'Thine be the glory'
22 'Since Jesus came into my heart'
23 'The Lord's my Shepherd'
24 'This little light of mine'
25 'And can it be…?'
26 'O God our help in ages past'
27 'Lord of all hopefulness'
28 'O for a closer walk with God'
29 'How sweet the name of Jesus sounds'
30 'O Jesus I have promised'
31 'Come down, O love divine'

**Acknowledgements:**
Original recordings made at Frog Studios, Cheshire and on location by **Gordon Lorenz.**

**Featuring…**
*Vocalists:* Ian Wallace, Jean Barrowman, Valerie Monese, Hero Douglas, John Delbridge.
*Choirs:* St George's Chapel Choir, Windsor Castle; Treorchy Male Voice Choir; The Choir of Guildford Cathedral; The Massed Choirs of Yorkshire; The Castleford Singers; The Gordon Lorenz Singers; Colwyn Bay Children's Choir.
*Musicians:* The Brighouse and Rastrick Brass Band, Matthew Freeman, Steve Millington, Barry Thompson.

*Engineers:* Mark Walker and Richard Scott.

Mastered at RAS Studios, Manchester. All recordings produced by **Gordon Lorenz.**